HOW TO RAISE & TRAIN AN

Alaskan Malamute

CHARLES J. BERGER

Distributed in the U.S.A. by T.F.H. Publications, Inc., 211 West Sylvania Avenue, P.O. Box 27, Neptune City, N.J. 07753; in England by T.F.H. (Gt. Britain) Ltd., 13 Nutley Lane, Reigate, Surrey; in Canada to the book store and library trade by Clarke, Irwin & Company, Clarwin House, 791 St. Clair Avenue West, Toronto 10, Ontario; in Canada to the pet trade by Rolf C. Hagen Ltd., 3225 Sartelon Street, Montreal 382, Quebec; in Southeast Asia by Y.W. Ong, 9 Lorong 3ſ Geylang, Singapore 14; in Australia and the south Pacific by Pe Imports Pty. Ltd., P.O. Box 149, Brookvale 2100, N.S.W., Australia. Published by T.F.H. Publications Inc. Ltd., The British Crown Colony of Hong Kong.

General illustrative photos by Louise
Brown van der Meid. Photos of champion
Malamutes are individually credited as to
owner and photographer wherever possible.

ISBN 0-87666-235-1

Contents

1. Introduction

DESCRIPTION

The Alaskan Malamute is a fairly large breed when compared to all the other breeds of dogs found in the world today. Being an active breed, also, it requires a good deal of exercise to remain in top condition. The Malamute probably does best in the country, where it has large areas of land at its disposal; however, it can easily adjust to life in the largest city if given adequate exercise. Besides its gentle manners and striking appearance, one must always remember that this breed was developed for work; therefore exercise plays a vital role in the all-round well-being of your Malamute.

An *average* weight and height for both male and female is sixty-seven pounds and twenty-two and one-half inches. Large Malamutes will tip the scales at eighty-five pounds, but over this is considered overweight. Considering that the Malamute was initially bred in Alaska, at the top of the world, it is no wonder that he has a thick, dense coat.

One of his most distinguishing features is his face markings— a sort of cap or mask. Malamutes come in various colors, but usually are black and white or a wolflike gray. Their eyes are also wolflike in appearance.

The Malamute has proven to have considerable tolerance for hot weather. Some of the largest kennels in the United States are in Georgia and southern California. Malamutes have also adapted well to the warm climates of Texas, Bermuda, and Puerto Rico. The North, however, is their native land and their ability to withstand cold is legend. Therefore, they can be kept outdoors in the coldest winter with a minimum of shelter.

PERSONALITY

The Malamute is an excellent companion for the outdoorsman. To walk, hike, or camp with a Malamute at your side is a wonderful feeling. The Malamute also makes an ideal children's pet. It is active, alert, friendly, and large enough to take the rough and tumble play that children, unfortunately, so often give to animals.

This powerful breed from the northernmost latitudes is well suited to be a house pet, too. Its only shortcoming, that of shedding its outer coat in the spring, is a minor one, because most of the shedding occurs over a relatively brief period. With daily, rigorous grooming during this shedding period, the problem is greatly minimized. What special qualities make the Malamute a house pet? It is a quiet dog. It seems to sense when it is time to withdraw, silently, to a corner. And the breed also has a certain dignity and proudness that evokes admiration everywhere.

RANK IN DOGDOM

Though the Malamute is grouped with the working dogs by the American Kennel Club, most of those found in the United States today are primarily companions. However, in recent years, there has been a gradual upsurge of a new winter sport in many areas of the country: *dog sled racing*. The Alaskan Malamute was bred initially to work in a harness, and this sport of racing is, needless to say, a natural for this breed. How many teams of dog sled racing Malamutes are there? It is difficult to say, but one thing is certain: more and more teams of Malamutes are joining the ranks of the sport every year.

HISTORY OF THE BREED

The Malamute was not the result of a deliberate planned effort, as was the Doberman Pinscher or Bullmastiff, and is therefore referred to as a *natural* breed. The Malamute was produced by a long, continuous process of culling dogs unable to meet the rigorous requirements of the North: the ability to serve as beasts of burden, hunting companions, and camp guards, and to survive under the most severe conditions of snow and cold. All these qualities are in today's Malamute. It is a fervent hope that modern breeders will maintain this breed as a fitting descendant of this background.

The name *Malamute* is derived from the Mahlemut Indians of Alaska, who are believed to have been extremely kind to their dogs. It was these Alaskan Indians who developed our breed, and it is in their honor that the Malamute has been named.

It is difficult to say when this breed was first developed, but both American and Russian writers of the nineteenth century wrote of the Malamute people who bred high-quality sled dogs. Surely it was not bred to a standard by these northern Indians in the same light as we think of a standard today. The "standard" that these Indians had was more or less dictated by ability and survival. Nature and the demands of the Indians culled the offspring of the existing stock through the many centuries, and today we have a hardy, thick-coated, powerful breed that we have chosen to call the *Alaskan Malamute.*

Ch. Apache Chief of Husky-Pak was bred by Hazel Wilton and is owned by Mr. & Mrs. Robert J. Zoller. Sire, Ch. Spawn's Alaska; dam, Chitina. The champion is shown being handled by Mr. Zoller.

This is a Siberian Husky. The markings of this breed and the Alaskan Malamute are similar.

Some authorities place the Malamute in a "Wolf-Spitz" classification. The primary members to this family are the Eskimo, Samoyed, and Siberian Husky. The resemblance to the Husky certainly is striking, especially the facial features. Other characteristics of this classification include that of carrying the tail over the back, short prick ears, and heavy fur.

The Alaskan Malamute was probably first brought to the United States around the turn of the century, but it is believed that these Malamutes eventually died out. Some years later, American sportsmen interested in developing this breed selected stock from remote Alaskan outposts and brought them back to this country, where they since have been perfected to conform to a written standard.

It was between the two World Wars that the Alaskan Malamute Club was formed, and the Alaskan Malamute received recognition from the American Kennel Club. Texts cite Mr. and Mrs. Milton

Ch. Sammey-ed II of Shining Star is owned and was bred by Winford G. Messier. Note the arctic characteristic of this Samoyed. Shown handling the champion is Thomas Flynn. Judge Earl T. Adair presents ribbon. Photo by Evelyn M. Shafer.

Ch. Tigara's Dortic Shag-Luck was bred and is owned by Mrs. Dorothy Dillingham. Sire, Ch. Tongass of Tigara; dam, Sno-Pak Kavik's Oonalik. The champion is being shown handled by Mrs. Dillingham, while judge Mrs. Lorna Dimidoff holds ribbon. Photo by Joan Ludwig.

The face markings of an Alaskan Malamute help to identify him.

J. Seeley as the most famous of Malamute breeders; dogs bred and trained by them accompanied various Antarctic expeditions.

During recent years the popularity of the Alaskan Malamute has increased substantially, but the Samoyeds and the Siberian Husky rank higher in American Kennel Club registrations.

THE SLED DOGS

The American Kennel Club presently recognizes three different breeds of dogs that are or were used as sled dogs. These are the Alaskan Malamute, Siberian Husky, and Samoyed. A fourth breed of sled dog, no longer recognized by the A.K.C., is the Eskimo dog.

The Alaskan Malamute is the largest of the A.K.C.-recognized sled dogs, and can easily be distinguished from the Samoyed. To the novice, however, there may be some difficulty in differentiating between the Alaskan Malamute and the Siberian Husky. The Siberian Husky is a smaller and lighter-boned animal, and should not exceed sixty pounds in weight. It is capable of pulling sleds at tremendous speeds for long distances.

The Malamute, which ranges up to eighty-five pounds in weight, is built for power and endurance. It is not as fast as the Siberian Husky, but its ability to pull heavy cargo long distances made it the freighting dog of the North. The Malamute also differs from the Husky by its broader head and different ear-carriage.

Sena-Lak's Rock of Alaska is owned by Stuart Mace.
Photo by Mr. & Mrs. A. J. DuBuis.

RESEMBLANCE TO THE WOLF

When walking a Malamute along a city street, one of the many comments is inevitably, "That looks like a wolf!"

It is true that the Malamute and the wolf have a superficial resemblance. The obliquely-set eyes of the wolf are very similar to the placement of the eyes in the Malamute. The general size and head structure are also similar. There are, however, many points which readily distinguish a Malamute from a wolf.

A Malamute, except when working, carries his tail over his back; the wolf is usually more slender and carries his tail low.

It is a well-established fact that there has been no cross-breeding with wolves in the maintenance of the modern Malamute breed. The Malamute is all dog and possesses a dog's dependable temperament.

2. Environment Suitable to the Breed

An Alaskan Malamute will fit well into the lives of people anywhere in the world. Even though he is an Alaskan dog, he'll adjust well to the balmy weather of Florida or California. Though an Alaskan Malamute may resemble a wolf at a great distance, this breed is as good a child's pet as any other breed of dog. Because of the Malamute's size, he could even be recommended for an untrained child.

KENNELS

The majority of Malamutes are kept outdoors and therefore a dog house is needed, if only to protect him from the heat. A dog house should be at least one and one-half times as large as the dog, and his sleeping quarters within the dog house should be twice as wide as the dog's height. A roofed-over porch, as wide as the dog house and from one and one-half to two feet deep, provides an outdoor shelter for the Malamute and makes the dog house much more serviceable.

A dog house with a draft-free sleeping area is especially good; this can be easily achieved by placing a short or partial wall inside the dog house perpendicular to the entrance. This divides the house into an entrance hall and a sleeping area. The dog then has to proceed from the entrance to the rear of the dog house and pass around the far end of the inside wall before turning into his sleeping quarters. An insulated dog house is advised because it minimizes the effects of both hot and cold weather. Ask your pet shop proprietor about the new insulated dog house which is now available.

To avoid dampness, the bottom of the dog house should never rest directly on the ground, but instead should be placed on legs or bricks set under each corner. The roof, which should be removable to allow thorough cleaning of the dog house, should be slanted so rain will run off. It is wise to cover the floor of the dog's sleeping quarters with some type of bedding material, such as cedar shavings (available at pet shops), to prevent sores and calluses from forming on the dog's legs and body.

Ch. Kelerak of Kobuk was bred by Earl and Natalie Norris, and is owned by Mr. & Mrs. Robert J. Zoller. Sire, Ch. Toro of Bras Coupe; dam, Helen of Bras Coupe. The champion is shown being handled by Mrs. Zoller.

Do not be surprised if your Malamute prefers to sleep outside of his dog house during a winter storm. This is quite natural for him, and you may rest assured that your pet is quite comfortable.

FOOD REQUIREMENTS

An average fifty-pound dog requires about thirty-five calories per pound per day, or a total of 1750 calories per day. A large eighty-five pound Malamute would therefore require 2975 calories per day. A hard-working dog will, of course, require more than an inactive house pet. A simple solution to the feeding of a Malamute is to follow the instructions printed on the package of the dog food you buy. You may add pan drippings, as most dry commercial foods are low in fat content. A dog's diet should contain a large amount of fat, but generally not in excess of fifteen percent of the total diet, except in the case of hard-working dogs who can utilize up to thirty percent. Fat serves as a storage site for vitamins A, D, E, and K, and also provides a high output of energy. Fat also slows the passage of food through the digestive tract allowing a more complete digestion of protein.

Do not allow more than thirty minutes per feeding. If the dog does not eat within this time, remove the food and do not feed again until the next regular scheduled feeding. This avoids the health hazard of spoiled food and teaches the dog to eat when served.

Fresh, clean water should be available at all times, except of course in winter when it would immediately freeze. If you live in regions where the temperature drops to below freezing and remains there for days or weeks at a time, offer your Malamute water several times a day. Chances are, however, that your Malamute will get most of his liquid requirements from the snow that he eats when thirsty.

EQUIPMENT

Other equipment which you will need to adequately house and keep a Malamute includes a collar, a sturdy chain if you do not have a run as part of the dog house, a leash, and grooming equipment. All of these things can be purchased at your pet shop.

EXERCISE

An Alaskan Malamute needs exercise. The amount of exercise required depends upon the role your dog is to play. If he is to take part in sled racing, a rigorous training program is recommended; however, should your Malamute be only a companion and a pet, then regular daily walks will be adequate to keep it healthy. Exercise is an important factor in a dog's life. It is a means of keeping his weight down, improving his appearance, and increasing his general well-being.

3. The New Puppy

INTRODUCING THE MALAMUTE PUPPY TO ITS NEW HOME

It is a strange and probably frightening world for the puppy on its first night away from its littermates, mother, and familiar surroundings. He will undoubtedly cry and raise quite a fuss as soon as it is left alone. To lessen this difficulty, feed the puppy a heavy meal before it is put to bed.

Though a loud-ticking clock is generally believed to comfort and relax a puppy, this is not a proven fact. If no great attention is paid to the whining, the puppy will probably abandon his efforts in a night or two. Make the puppy as comfortable as possible. Give him a bed of his own. A large corrugated carton will serve adequately for the first few days. It may also be helpful to give the puppy some article of yours or one that you have handled. Your scent on this article may relax the puppy and make him feel more secure.

CHOOSING THE MALAMUTE

It is important to see a reputable breeder or pet shop once you have decided to own a Malamute. A clean kennel with proper facilities will usually mean healthy, well-nourished puppies.

If the Malamute is to be a pet, it is advisable to purchase a puppy of two to four months of age. As the puppy grows, an important bond is established between you and the dog. You act as a prime influence in its development and consequently determine the kind of adult animal it will be.

The A.K.C., upon request, will send you a list of Malamute breeders in your area. Do not under any circumstances purchase a puppy from a breeder who does not allow you ownership, on approval, for at least twenty-four hours, so the puppy may be examined by a veterinarian. Any reliable kennel will grant you this consideration.

A dog's normal temperature is approximately 101.5 degrees Fahrenheit. Though excitement may raise this to a somewhat higher level, do not select a puppy whose temperature is more than 102 degrees. Other signs of ill health are coughing, diarrhea, mucous discharge from the eyes or nose, and skin rashes.

In general, pick an alert puppy rather than a cowering, timid, or listless one.

For show-dog considerations, choose the puppy that is neither the largest nor the smallest of the litter.

MALE OR FEMALE

The decision of what sex to purchase is a problem all prospective dog owners face. There are advantages and disadvantages to both sexes.

The male Malamute, due to his slightly larger size, has perhaps a more impressive appearance. In a male, the heavy broad-boned head, which easily distinguishes him from a female, should always be evident. The male Malamute tends to be more aggressive toward other male dogs, and is probably just a bit more difficult to train.

The female, in general, is more gentle and less inclined to wander. She is not as large as the male and will fit into a smaller home more easily. The estrous cycle (or heat period), which occurs approximately every six months and lasts about three weeks (indicated by a slight vaginal discharge), may be considered a disadvantage in owning a female. The compensatory joy of raising a litter of puppies, however, generally counterbalances this.

TRAINING THE NEW PUPPY

The young puppy can readily be taught the meaning of "No." Even his mother did not let him get away with everything. Do not, however, expect instantaneous and unwavering obedience; the puppy, after all, is still a puppy.

It is not possible to overstress the importance of consistency: when you say "No," *mean it*. Do not give the command several times and then allow the dog to continue what it is doing, simply because it is too much effort to enforce your commands. Be prepared to back up your orders, or do not give them.

It is, however, undesirable to be a martinet and overtrain your dog. Excessive scolding and restraint may result in the unpleasant sight of a cringing, fearful dog every time you look at or reach for it. A dog, especially a young puppy, should be allowed certain liberties. Use the command "No" wisely and with discretion, and not every time the dog turns his head—but when you give the command make sure it is always obeyed.

WALKING ON LEASH

One of the basic things a well-disciplined dog must know is proper conduct while on a leash (as distinct from "heeling"). The dog should not pull, bolt, or hang back, though he should, of course, be allowed a certain degree of liberty when taken to his relief area,

If you don't want your Alaskan Malamute to beg at your table, never permit him to do so.

If your Alaskan Malamute is to be a house pet, then have a bed waiting for him when you bring him home.

for dogs want to sniff and investigate a spot before making use of it.

For your Malamute puppy, a rounded leather collar and the standard length leash, three feet long, are quite suitable as walking accoutrements (people professionally associated with the world of dogs refer to a "leash" as a "lead"). A harness may also be used, but it makes control of the dog much more difficult.

A good collar size for your young puppy is one that can be gently tightened to the last hole. This size will allow for the puppy's continued growth. The collar, however, should not be worn this tightly, but, instead, slightly loose to prevent chafing and choking. For the adult dog, the collar should fit comfortably when tightened to the middle hole. If you wish to buy a collar without the dog being present, and still obtain the correct size, you should determine before-hand the circumference of the dog's neck by using a tape measure or a length of string.

Allow the puppy to smell and examine his new collar. Slip it loosely on and off his neck several times, leaving it in place for progressively longer periods. Finally, leave it on. Allow the puppy, also, to sniff and become familiar with his leash before you attach it to his collar. Once the leash is in place, allow the puppy to run about without any restraint until he realizes the leash is nothing to fear.

When walking, each time the puppy pulls on the leash respond with a sharp but gentle tug. If the puppy lingers behind, however,

Ch. Tamerack of Tigara was bred by Dorothy Dillingham and is owned by Roy W. Truchon, shown handling the champion. Sire, Ch. Sno-Pak Kavik's Oopik; dam, Calaeno of Tigara. Photo by William Brown.

your tugging on the leash may only result in the puppy's sitting and actively resisting your efforts. In this event, try to coax him, with suitable words, into following the directional pull of the leash. If he persists, gently drag him along; when he starts to walk, praise him.

Puppies usually learn their leash manners in a short time, but puppies are young animals and allowances must be made for their playfulness. Give them a certain amount of liberty and do not expect absolute precision.

Obedience-training collars and leashes are discussed in Chapter 5.

HOUSE-TRAINING

House-breaking, as distinguished from paper-training, is almost impossible in puppies less than four months of age. They simply lack sufficient control of their bowel and bladder movements. If, however, you have the time and quick access to the outside (not a neighbor's lawn), you may try to impress upon your puppy the desired association of the out-of-doors with the daily eliminations.

If you don't want your Alaskan Malamute to sit on furniture, never permit him to do so.

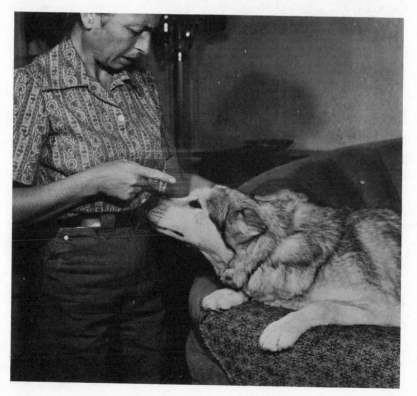

This means taking the puppy outside when you awaken in the morning, after each feeding, after heavy play or exercise, and before retiring at night. Each of these excursions should last at least fifteen minutes to give the puppy ample time. This practice, therefore, can be rather time consuming.

For your convenience, for the health of the puppy in very cold and damp weather, and for the protection of the household rugs, paper-training as the initial step in house-breaking is highly recommended. A grown dog that is both paper-broken and house-broken is a great advantage to apartment-house dwellers, live-alone workers, and travelers. Paper-training, however, has two aspects that may be considered objectionable: (1) the almost unending presence of urine-soaked paper in the house, (2) "defiling" the "sacredness" of the home, which tends to make later attempts at house-breaking more difficult.

Living with a dog, however, like living with other people, requires the acceptance of certain household inconveniences. If a chewed slipper or a spot on the rug works you into a fury, or if you do not care enough to devote sufficient time to a dog, you should not own one.

Ch. Husky-Pak Marclar's Seoux was bred by C. W. and Mary Cramer. The champion is owned by Mr. & Mrs. Robert J. Zoller, and is shown being handled by Mrs. Zoller. Sire, Ch. Apache Chief of Husky-Pak; dam, Ch. Cheyenne of Husky-Pak.

PAPER-TRAINING

Paper-training can begin when the puppy is eight weeks old, but do not expect instantaneous perfection. The basic procedure is as follows:

It is best to establish and keep a specific part of the house as the puppy's "territory." The territory should have linoleum rather than a rug or bare-wood flooring. It should not be located in the main stream of family traffic, yet it should not be so isolated as to remove the dog from all human contact. If space allows, the kitchen or breakfast nook—or a part thereof—is usually an ideal site. Confinement to this area can be achieved either by tieing the puppy with his leash or a cord to some sturdy object or, preferably, by partitioning off the territory with a gate or some obstacle across the doorway entrance.

Cover the entire floor of the territory with at least two layers of newspaper. After one or more days, the puppy will localize his attentions to one part of the territory. To speed up and encourage the use of a particular location, it is a good idea to leave a little of the used paper at that location. Once a definite spot is established, reduce the area covered by the newspapers by eliminating those furthest from the point of use. You are now leaving room for error, and errors will occur. Your pet shop has house-breaking scents to help you train your Malamute puppy.

If you are with the puppy either in another room or near his territory, and you notice him circling, suddenly begin to sniff the floor, or squatting, quickly but gently place him on the newspaper. Whenever the puppy uses the paper, whether voluntarily or placed there by you, bestow lavish praise and petting upon him. If you do not catch him in time, scold him and immediately place him on the paper. Do not beat him or, under any condition, rub his nose in it. Scoldings must be given *only during* or *immediately after* the mistake, for after any lapse of time at all the scoldings will not be associated with the misdeed, and only confusion and fear will result.

Gradually, as the puppy's training progresses, reduce the newspaper-covered area to the minimum size necessary for adequate service. You may allow the puppy greater freedom in the house. Off-paper mistakes will occur, and you must be prepared to accept these as inevitable. Do not leave the puppy alone, even temporarily, in a room without newspaper on the floor, for unavoidable accidents may occur and set back the whole training process.

When the puppy is four months old, he has usually developed sufficient muscular control to begin house-breaking. At this point, you must decide whether you want a completely house-broken dog or a combination paper- and house-broken animal. If the former is decided upon, all newspaper must be permanently removed during the day. Leaving newspapers down during the day, in case of an emergency, may be a convenience to you, but it will simply prolong,

Ch. Arctic Storm of Husky-Pak is owned by Mr. & Mrs. Robert J. Zoller. She was bred by Hazel Wilton. Sire, Ch. Spawn's Alaska; dam, Chitina. In one litter alone, Ch. Arctic Storm of Husky-Pak produced five champions.

hinder, and possibly nullify all your house-breaking efforts. Until the puppy develops more control, however, or if you wish a combination-trained dog, newspapers can be left on the floor during the night.

HOUSE-BREAKING

House-breaking requires a completely new training process, and hence the following instructions can be used with either paper-broken dogs or dogs with no previous training whatever.

The first step in house-breaking is to establish a regular outing schedule. For the young puppy, this should be in the early morning, at night before retiring, and after each feeding. It is also advisable to walk a puppy after heavy play or exercise and after awakening from a nap. This generally boils down to the fact that you should walk your young puppy about every three hours. Adult dogs should be walked no less than twice a day, but even this is an unhappy and uncomfortable restriction. Three times a day would be much better.

The second step is to take advantage of the average dog's dislike of soiling the immediate area of his living quarters or anywhere in which he is closely confined. Thus, when you cannot keep a constant watch on the puppy while he is in the house, tie or barricade him within a small area, such as near his bed or the vicinity of the bathroom sink. This will induce the puppy to make an effort at self-restraint, which will both strengthen and improve his control and allow you to adhere more closely to a regular outing schedule.

If he does err while in the house, scold him, but only *during* or *immediately following* the mistake, not sometime after. For an effective scolding, the puppy should be kept at or brought back to the spot he has soiled and restrained there by holding his collar or the scruff of his neck. The scolding should be done in an angry voice using such expressions as *"No! You bad dog! No!"* You may, if you wish, as long as the puppy is restrained in place, swat him on his rear quarters with your bare hand. Moderate your blows so as to give only a degree of pain or smarting; never allow them to become forceful enough to bruise or injure the puppy. Rolled-up newspaper may also be efficient, but its use in paper-training may lead to confusion in the dog's mind as to the desirability of his close association with newspapers.

Punching or kicking the dog or pushing his nose into the mess is outright cruelty and does not hasten or improve his training; indeed, it may result in unwanted complications. Never attempt to strike at the dog, either with a newspaper or your hand, while he is free and can dodge and run away. Once the dog learns he can run away from punishment, he will tend to become hand-shy and make training all the more difficult. If it is at all possible, the dog should be taken outside after he has been scolded for soiling in the house.

Following a routine, which is basically repeating the same thing over and over again, enables the puppy to learn more quickly. Therefore, along with a regular feeding and walking schedule, always use the same door, if there is more than one, when leaving the house, and always walk along the same route. When the puppy utilizes the gutter—*not the sidewalk, please!*—praise and pet him. Show him clearly how pleased you are. Gradually, the number of outings may be reduced and the puppy given greater freedom in the house.

4. Grooming the Malamute

The Malamute should have a very dense undercoat and a coarse medium-length outer coat. A good stiff brush plus a comb with wide-set teeth are the primary grooming tools. The Malamute should be brushed vigorously several times a week. Brushing stimulates the circulation and increases the luster of the coat. The Malamute seldom needs a bath if proper care is given to his coat, if he doesn't get dirty. Like other sled dog breeds, he lacks an offensive doggy odor.

BATHING

The frequency of bathing depends upon the individual dog and specific circumstances. In order to have a clean dog some type of bath must be given. A dog can be given either a wet, semi-wet, or a dry bath. All of these cleaning agents can be purchased at your pet shop. Never use human soaps or shampoos on your Malamute. They may be too strong and too heavily scented.

Dogs may be bathed in cold weather, contrary to a popular line of thought, as long as the dog is kept in a warm, draft-free place until thoroughly dried. Puppies may also be bathed, but try to avoid bathing a puppy before it is five months old; if a puppy requires a bath, however, give him one.

When bathing the dog, begin by wetting him thoroughly with warm water; then apply soap or shampoo to the head region and gradually, with a massaging motion, work down toward the rear of the body. This is important, for if you begin at the middle or rear of the dog's body, fleas and other parasites will run forward and hide in the ears and other head openings.

Work carefully so as not to get soap in the dog's eyes. Some authorities recommend placing a drop of castor oil or mineral oil into each eye before the soaping, to form a protective film against possible irritation. Placing a wad of absorbent cotton in each of the dog's ears has also been recommended. An effective tear-less dog shampoo is available at your pet shop.

Follow the manufacturer's instructions on the soap or shampoo container. Some manufacturers recommend keeping the suds on the dog for at least five minutes to maximize the insecticidal effect. (Another reason why you shouldn't use human soaps or shampoos!)

Rinse the dog thoroughly with warm water, for any soap left on the skin may cause irritation. It is best to dry the dog with towels rather than letting him dry in the air, and though it is less effort to let the dog shake himself several times before toweling, it may

An Alaskan Malamute can be an ideal child's pet.

be advisable to place a towel on the dog prior to any shaking to absorb excess water and avoid having yourself splattered and drenched. To induce the dog to shake, blow gently in one of his ears. Do not overdo this, however, as it appears to greatly annoy the dog.

Mechanical hot air dryers are sold by pet shops to facilitate fast drying.

EARS

The ears can be cleaned in any of several ways. If the ear is in very bad condition, with hard accumulations of wax and dirt, it is best to flush the ear by placing several drops of peroxide, propylene glycol, or a mixture of ether and alcohol in the ear to dissolve the waxy secretions. The ear can then be cleaned with a moistened cotton swab. (Q-tips—cardboard sticks preferred.) If the ear is not very dirty, the cotton swab can be dampened with any of the following: peroxide, propylene glycol, an ether and alcohol mixture, rubbing alcohol, mineral oil, olive oil, or baby oil, all of which act to soften and loosen the wax. It is wise not to probe the swab any deeper than you can see. Be sure to hold the dog's head steady, for any sudden movement by the dog may ram the swab inward and injure him. Your pet shop has special ear drops to help you keep your Malamute's ears healthy.

THE CLAWS

If the Malamute is given a sufficient amount of exercise, especially over hard ground, its claws will be worn down to a satisfactory length, and little care is necessary.

A house dog, with insufficient exercise, usually needs periodic cutting of the claws. Overly long claws can cause problems by spreading the pads of the foot or by actually growing into the pads and causing lameness.

In clipping the dog's claws, great care should be taken not to cut into the quick (blood vessel). Use special clippers made especially for dog's claws.

It is wise to observe an experienced person at this task before you attempt it yourself. Have your pet shop demonstrate the "Dog Nail Clippers" for you.

THE TEETH

Dogs are not usually subjected to the common types of tooth decay that so often afflict man. Proper diet is an important safeguard of good teeth. The dog's teeth should be periodically inspected, and any debris found lodged between the teeth removed.

As a dog ages, tartar (yellowish crusty deposits) may form on the teeth. A veterinarian can easily and painlessly remove these accumulations, which otherwise may invade the gums and produce abscesses.

Loose teeth in old dogs have a tendency to become infected and should be removed by a veterinarian. A dog on a proper diet and in satisfactory condition should have very few dental problems.

When light tartar accumulations first appear on the teeth, much of it can be wiped off with a cloth. A large hide or nylon bone given to the dog as a toy for chewing exercise will remove minor tartar accumulations and help keep the teeth white.

Ch. Tigara's Torch of Arctica is shown being handled by breeder-owner Mrs. Dorothy Dillingham. Sire, Ch. Tigara's Arctic Explorer; dam, Tigara's Winsome Witch. Photo by Joan Ludwig.

5. Training

OBEDIENCE TRAINING

The absolute minimum or, in actuality, all that a dog really needs in discipline training is obedience to the commands of *"No,"* *"Come,"* *"Sit,"* and *"Stay."* If your dog obeys only these four commands in the proper manner, he will be head and shoulders above the average dog. With the addition of the commands *"Down"* and *"Heel,"* you will be able to control your dog in almost any circumstance, increase your pride of ownership, and greatly enhance the master-dog relationship. More advanced training, however, can add markedly to this situation.

No training attempts whatever should be made with puppies less than three months of age. Indeed, few puppies are ready for real training before they reach six months. It is best, therefore, to wait until the puppy is at least this old before beginning regular obedience training. Paper-training and house-breaking, obedience to the command *"No,"* and incidental association with the command *"Come"* are notable exceptions to this rule. Many training classes will not accept puppies less than eight months of age, and a number of authorities consider nine months as the minimum age. Premature attempts at training a puppy can result in a tense, nervous, and excitable dog.

Recent scientific studies, however, have indicated that, under certain conditions, "play-training" not only can, but *should* begin at seven weeks of age. From seven to twelve weeks of age, according to these findings, the trainer should establish a bond between himself and the puppy; during the interval, an understanding of, but not a disciplined obedience to, the commands *"No,"* *"Sit,"* *"Stay,"* and *"Come"* can be learned. Regular discipline training can then be taught by sixteen weeks of age. These experimental studies and techniques are most interesting and may prove of great value, but their proof should be left to the professional dog trainer.

Older dogs, despite ideas to the contrary, can also be trained.

Training sessions should last about fifteen minutes each, or even less in the beginning, and not more than twenty minutes. One or two training periods per day, given at regularly scheduled times, several hours apart, are quite adequate. Training should be conducted away from any outside distraction that would interfere with gaining and keeping the dog's attention. The dog must also be made to understand that training sessions are serious occasions and not a time for play; the execution of a command is not a game to be indulged in only when the puppy is in the mood.

When giving commands, to avoid later confusion in obedience trials where other trainers are present, it is best to preface all commands (except "*Stay*") with the dog's name, as "*Storm, Heel!*"

It might be well to repeat here the earlier warning against overtraining: excessive strictness and too many scoldings may produce a cringing dog instead of a trusting companion.

Training sessions should not be held immediately after the dog has eaten or has had a quantity of water. At least one-half hour after drinking and one and one-half to two hours after eating should be allowed.

In training, a metal slip chain or, as it is more honestly known, a *choke collar*, is best. A choke collar permits quick application of pressure and its immediate release. This is a decided aid in restraining a dog and in telegraphing your commands. There is also a spike collar available, which has inward-projecting prongs, but its use is not as highly recommended.

Do not get too narrow a chain, for it may cut into the dog's skin. The proper length slip chain is one having about three or four inches of excess length when the collar is cinched snugly around the dog's neck. To form the slip-chain collar from the open chain, merely pass a loop of the chain through one of the end rings (this is actually done by dropping the links of the chain through one ring), and then slip this loop over the dog's head.

You must know the correct method of placing a choke collar on a dog so that it will slacken immediately when pressure is released. This is an important requisite, for both the training and the well-being of the dog. There *is* a correct way to place the choke collar, but it is important to realize that this placement remains correct only as long as the dog remains on one side of you. In formal obedience training, the dog is kept on the trainer's left, and this custom is generally followed by most dog owners. The following description of how to correctly place the choke collar will, therefore, pertain to the dog kept at your left side, and it will be correct only as long as the dog stays on your left side: With the dog at your left side, place the slip chain over his head so the loose, dangling ring, to which you fasten the leash, is on the dog's right side. If placed correctly, a pull on the leash, while both end-rings are below the dog's neck, will cause the formation of a V in the collar with the remaining end-ring in the crook of this bend. If the collar has been placed incorrectly, a pull on the leash will not result in this V-formation. In the usual walking position, when the dog pulls on the leash, the slip collar will slide around so that both end-rings will be above his neck rather than below it. In this reversed position, with the dog still at your left side, the V-bend should no longer be formed. If the V-bend is present, the collar has been positioned incorrectly.

A training leash (or lead) should be approximately six feet long to provide adequate maneuverability for the trainer. It should be made of flat leather or webbing. A rounded-leather leash is difficult to hold, and a chain lead may cut into the trainer's hand. A thin clothes line or similar rope, about fifty feet long, will also be required.

If the dog is to be taught in the usual left-of-trainer position, hold the handle of the leash, and any excess length of leash in the form of a loop, in the right hand. The left hand is used to grasp the straight part of the leash a short distance from the dog. The left hand is used to control or pet the dog, and the right hand to adjust the length of leash needed. The leash should be held slack at all times, except when correcting the dog.

Obedience-training classes, and most instruction books, begin with "heeling" as the first phase of training. This is because the subsequent training program is in relation to heeling and the heeling position. If, however, you are not concerned with formal obedience training, or if you do not particularly care if the dog walks at your left side with his head close to your left knee or not (so long as it acts properly while walking on a leash), and you do not wish to take on the additional task of training the dog to heel, you may skip the heeling training entirely.

SIT

To teach the dog to sit on command, give the command "*Sit*," as you pull steadily upward on the leash with one hand and press downward on the dog's hindquarters with your other. If the dog resists, a sharp slap on the hindquarters, while keeping the leash high and taut, will provide an additional incentive. When the dog sits, regardless of whether it was of his own accord or due to your physical urgings, praise and pet him, and occasionally give him a tidbit. After a number of lessons, the dog should sit quickly on command. The distance between you and the dog should gradually be increased in order to train the dog to sit on command when he is some distance from you. Hand signals can be given simultaneously with the vocal commands, and then, gradually the vocal commands lessened until the dog is obeying the hand signal alone. In formal obedience training, the hand-signal for "*Sit*" is to extend the arm, palm up, and then quickly bend the fingers upward.

STAY

The command "*Stay*" is a very important command, and one that seems most impressive to the average person. Training is begun by holding the leash in the prescribed manner with the dog at your left side.

Have the dog sit on command. Step forward slowly, starting

with your right foot (if you are not going to enter the dog in formal obedience training, you may use either foot—see *"Heeling"*), turn and face the dog. Give him the command *"Stay!"* (in formal obedience training it is *"Sit-and-Stay"*) and, at the same time, reinforce it with the appropriate hand signal: arm extended and the turned-back palm placed in front of the dog's muzzle, as if you were going to push his nose in. You may, at first, have to keep the dog in place by holding him with your left hand when you walk away from him, or tapping him on the muzzle with one or two fingers.

If the dog begins to move as you stand facing him, snap the leash upward and give the commands *"Sit, Stay!"* Gradually, you may step back farther and farther from the dog until the full length of the leash is reached. At this stage, you can begin a slow circling of the dog after he has been told to sit and stay. Slow movement is important, for dogs lunge instinctively after something moving rapidly, and you want to discourage this. The dog should not be allowed to turn his body around to follow your movements. To prevent this, you may, at first, have to hold his head in a forward position with your hand as you walk around him.

Later, you can leave the leash on the ground when you walk from him or around him. Always be prepared to correct the dog when he breaks the command. If he moves off, bring him back to the exact place he has left, and repeat the command. Gradually, move farther and farther from him, and make him stay in place for longer and longer periods. Finally, you may walk out of sight, preferably to a location where you can still watch him. If he starts to move, repeat the command to stay. Have the dog sit and stay by himself for one or more minutes, and later for five to ten minutes. Always reward the dog when he obeys. Show him that you are aware of and appreciate his efforts and achievements.

COME ON COMMAND

A young puppy can be taught to come when called by rewarding him with praise, petting, and an occasional tidbit every time he responds to the call as long as he is not punished when he does not come or when he obeys very slowly, for then he will begin to associate this command as preceding a scolding and will retreat rather than approach when this command is given. This informal voluntary compliance, however, is not sufficient. It must be impressed upon the puppy, when he is old enough, and the older dog as well, that obedience to the command *"Come!"* is not dependent solely upon materialistic reward, but is, rather, a mandatory duty.

To convey this idea, make the dog sit and stay, and then back slowly away the full length of the leash. At the command *"Come,"* yank the leash sharply but gently toward you. If the dog refuses to budge, yank the leash again and repeat the command. Continue doing this until the dog is in front of you. At this point, give the command to sit, and then reward him with praise, petting, and an occasional tidbit. Once the dog begins to grasp the meaning of

"Come," you can make use of the fifty-foot line. With the line secured to the dog, you can vary the training distance by letting the dog wander away or by having him sit and stay while you back away. At these various distances, you repeat the training procedure outlined above. When the dog obeys consistently from a fifty-foot distance, you may dispense with the line and continue training without any leash whatever. Train without the line only in a safe place where a sudden unexpected dash by the dog will not carry him under the wheels of a speeding car.

A word of caution: *Never* give the dog the command to *"Come"* to punish him for anything he has done. He should never be punished when he obeys this command, regardless of what else he has done, or you will inhibit his obedience to this command. If you have to punish him for something, go to him!

HEELING

"Heeling" is actually a two phase command: one, to get the dog seated in the proper position at your left side when you are standing still; and two, to keep him at your left side while you are walking.

It is best to begin heeling with the walking phase. Keep the dog at your left side, with the leash held in the prescribed manner. You may begin walking with either foot; in formal obedience training, however, the trainer begins with his left foot. Starting off with the right foot is used only when the dog has been told to stay in place. Walk at a rather rapid pace; keep the leash slack, but yank it to correct the dog. Try to keep the dog's head near your left knee. Each time the dog pulls too far ahead or lags too far behind, tug on the leash and give the command *"Heel!"* or *"Storm, Heel!"* To make the meaning of the command more clear to the dog and to keep his attention, vary your speed and direction of walking. Try reversing your course or turning to one side suddenly, jerking the leash sharply as you do; walk in a circle, both to the left and right; or walk in a figure "8." If the dog gets in your way on these turns, nudge him with your knee. Keep repeating the command to heel. Do not allow the dog to play.

The *"sitting"* heel. After the dog has gotten the idea of heeling at your side as you walk, command him to sit every time you come to a halt. After a while, the dog will learn to sit whenever you stop walking. The next step is to get the dog to come to the "sitting" heel position from a point other than at your side. This is best done by facing the seated dog while holding the leash in the prescribed manner. Give the command *"Heel,"* and then walk briskly toward the dog and pass it on your left side. The pull of the leash will cause the dog to turn and follow you. As soon as the dog has swung into position, halt and give the command to *"Sit."* Repeat this training until the dog follows you automatically without the guiding pull of the leash, on the command of *"Heel."* You may then vary the training by walking several steps backwards as you give the command, pulling the dog after you, then moving forward until the dog has turned and is at your side in the heel position. Gradually, take fewer steps backward and let the sharp tugs of the leash, accompanied by command *"Heel"* replace your stepping backward. In time, both the "walking" and "sitting" heel will be obeyed without the necessity of a leash.

DOWN

Training the dog to drop to his stomach on command can be done in several ways. All begin with the dog in a sitting position.

Situate yourself alongside the dog. At the command *"Down,"* place your arm behind the dog's front legs and push them forward while you simultaneously push down with your other hand on the dog's back between the shoulder blades.

Another method is to place yourself in front of the seated dog, and on the command *"Down,"* grasp one front leg in each hand and pull the legs forward. Or stand facing the dog, holding the leash, in a loop if it is necessary to shorten it, in your left hand. On the command *"Down!"*, place your right foot on the leash and gently force it to the ground. This will bring the dog into the correct down position.

Repeat any *one* of these procedures until the dog obeys the command without any physical urging.

To get the dog to "sit" from the "down" position, give the command *"Sit!"* and tug sharply, but gently, upward with the leash.

6. Breeding and Reproduction

The breeding and reproduction of the dog is a topic worthy of numerous volumes. Several excellent books written for the laymen are in most libraries, and should be read by those who want to pursue this topic beyond the brief accounting given here.

The Alaskan Malamute reaches sexual maturity at from approximately six to twelve months of age. This is variable and could extend beyond these limits. The female normally comes into heat twice a year. The heat periods are characterized by varying degrees of vaginal bleeding. Each heat period lasts for approximately three weeks. It is during this time (usually from the ninth to the thirteenth day after the appearance of the bloody discharge) that the bitch will receive the male.

It is not wise to breed the bitch in her first heat period, for she is still not fully grown and needs all the nutrients she receives for her own body-building processes. In general, it is best to wait until the female is at least eighteen months old before breeding her.

SELECTING THE STUD

Extreme care should be taken in selecting the Malamute stud. Don't use a stud just because it happens to reside in your area, or because the stud fee is low. Always breed to the best stud available, as indicated by show-ring records, temperament, and general conformity to the Malamute standard. Do not breed to a nervous, ill-tempered dog, under any circumstances. In fact, for the good of the breed, do not mate your bitch unless she is a representative specimen of the breed and of sound temperament and disposition. This will insure the maintenance of the Alaskan Malamute's fine qualities.

CONCEPTION

To increase the likelihood of conception, it is probably best to mate the female twice, the two matings separated by a day. The ninth and eleventh days after the onset of the vaginal discharge often provide the greatest chances for pregnancy.

The exact time to breed can best be determined by the female's receptive attitudes to males, or by a vaginal smear (veterinary microscopic examination of the vaginal fluid).

Have your veterinarian check the female well before delivery is due and ask him to advise you on a proper diet and supplements during the periods of pregnancy and weaning.

WHELPING

The Alaskan Malamute almost never has difficulty in whelping. If labor seems unduly difficult, however, do not hesitate to call your veterinarian. This is a precaution of prime importance that can save the lives of the puppies as well as the bitch.

A whelping-box should be available well before delivery time, to allow the female to accustom herself to it. The whelping-box should be approximately five feet square in size.

It is of the utmost importance that the brood female be lean and in excellent condition before breeding. It is a good idea to have the female checked for worms and, if necessary, wormed before breeding or within three weeks after breeding. Revaccination (booster) for distemper and hepatitis is strongly recommended.

MATING

The male dog's penis has a bulbous enlargement at its base and, in addition, like a number of other mammals, contains a bone. When mating occurs, pressure on the penis causes a reflex action that fills the bulb with blood, swelling it to about five times its normal size within the female. This locks or "ties" the two animals together. After ejaculation, the animals usually remain tied for fifteen to thirty minutes, but they may separate very quickly or remain together for one or more hours. When the dogs are thus tied, you should not allow the female to sit or turn and bite at the male, for he may be injured. Keep the female up, if necessary, by hand or knee support, and muzzle her if she shows a tendency to bite. In the tied position, the male will often turn around so that both dogs are tail to tail; in this position, they will part as soon as the bulb reduces in size. You may bring the male to this reverse position by lifting his forelegs off the female and dropping them to one side of her, then lifting the male's hind leg of the opposite side and bringing it across the female's back.

CONTRACTS AND SHIPPING

In breeding arrangements, the general procedure is to bring the female to the male, or stud. If the stud is located some distance away, this may mean shipping your female. If so, the female should be shipped before the seventh day of her estrous cycle to allow her to become accustomed to her new surroundings and be with the stud at the most expeditious time. For relatively short journeys, railway express (REA) or air cargo is quite satisfactory. For long distances, time should be considered and the female should be shipped by air express (as freight on passenger planes) or even by direct flight if the owner of the stud is able and willing to meet the plane. Many breeders recommend not shipping by air cargo on Friday, Saturday, or Sunday, for a flight may be cancelled and the dog stranded over the weekend.

The dog's shipping crate should be sturdy and large enough to prevent cramping. A water dish should be securely affixed to the inside. If the trip will take a day or less, the inclusion of food is not necessary; for longer intervals, sealed foods should be attached to or placed inside the crate. REA Express personnel will feed and care for your dog on the trip. All pertinent instructions regarding the handling of the dog, including your name, address, and telephone number so you can be reached in cases of unforeseen delay or other events, should be indelibly inscribed on, or permanently attached to, the crate. If you are shipping interstate, you should apprise yourself of the health certificate requirements by consulting the shipping agency, the AAA, or your health department. Most airlines rent suitable shipping crates for dogs.

Either as the owner of the female or the stud, the fees and any supplementary agreement—such as a reservice of the female, at no charge, at her next heat, in case this mating proves fruitless—should be in writing. Stud fees are usually the going price of a puppy, and many owners of stud dogs may request the pick of the litter instead of cash payment. Stud fees may also be much higher, especially if the stud is a champion or a known sire of champions.

STUD FOR HIRE

If you are the owner of a male dog, and wish to employ him as a stud, you can advertise his availability in show programs, dog magazines, and the local newspaper or pet shop. It is unlikely, however, that your stud will be in demand unless he is a champion. Male dogs can be used as studs any time after reaching puberty, but many breeders do not utilize a male until he is between twelve and eighteen months of age.

GENETICS

Any person attempting to breed dogs should have a basic understanding of the transmission of traits or characteristics from the parents to the offspring and some familiarity with the more widely used genetic terms that he will probably encounter.

Inheritance, fundamentally, is due to the existence of microscopic units, known as GENES, present in the cells of all individuals. Genes somehow control the biochemical reactions that occur within the embryo or adult organism. This control results in changing or guiding the development of the organism's characteristics. A "string"

Ch. Cherokee of Husky-Pak is shown handled by the breeder-owner Robert J. Zoller. Sire, Ch. Toro of Bras Coupe; dam, Ch. Arctic Storm of Husky-Pak. The champion holds many all-time breed records.

of attached genes is known as a CHROMOSOME. With a few important exceptions, every chromosome has a partner chromosome carrying a duplicate or equivalent set of genes. Each gene, therefore, has a partner gene, known as an ALLELE. The number of different pairs of chromosomes present in the cells of the organism varies with the type of organism: a certain kind of parasitic worm has only one pair, a certain fruit fly has four different pairs, man has twenty-three different pairs, and the dog has thirty-nine different pairs per cell. Heredity is obviously a very complex matter.

In the simplest form of genetic inheritance, one particular gene and its duplicate, or allele, on the partner chromosome controls a single characteristic. The presence of freckles in the human skin, for example, is believed to be due to the influence of a single pair of genes.

Each cell of the body contains the specific number of paired chromosomes characteristic of the organism. Because each type of gene is present on both chromosomes of a chromosome pair, each type of gene is therefore present in duplicate (2). The fusion of a sperm cell from the male with an egg cell from the female, as occurs in fertilization, should therefore result in offspring having a quadruplicate number (4) of each type of gene. Mating of these individuals would then produce progeny having an octuplicate number (8) of each type of gene, and so on. This, however, is normally prevented by a special process. When ordinary body cells prepare to divide to form more tissue, each pair of chromosomes duplicates itself so that there are four partner chromosomes of each kind instead of only two. When the cell divides, two of the four partners, or one pair, go into each new cell. This process, known as MITOSIS, insures that each new body cell contains the proper number of chromosomes. Reproductive cells (sperm cells and egg cells), however, undergo a special kind of division known as MEIOSIS. In meiosis, the chromosome pairs do *not* duplicate themselves, and thus when the reproductive cells reach the final dividing stage only one chromosome, or one-half of the pair, goes into each new reproductive cell. Each reproductive cell, therefore, has only half the normal number of chromosomes. These are referred to as HAPLOID cells in contrast to DIPLOID cells with the full number of chromosomes. When the haploid sperm cell fuses with the haploid egg cell in fertilization, the resulting offspring has the normal (diploid) number of chromosomes.

If both partner genes, or alleles, affect the trait in an identical manner, the genes are said to be HOMOZYGOUS, but if one affects the character in a manner different from the other gene or allele, the genes are said to be HETEROZYGOUS. For example, in the pair of genes affecting eye color, if each gene of the pair produces blue eyes, the genes (and also the person carrying the genes) are said to be homozygous for blue eyes. If, however, one gene of the pair produces blue eyes, while the other gene or allele produces brown eyes, they are said to be heterozygous. The presence of heterozygous genes

raises the question of whether the offspring have blue eyes or brown eyes, which in turn introduces another genetic principle: DOMINANCE and RECESSIVENESS.

If one gene of a pair can block the action of its partner or allele while still producing its own affect, that gene is said to be dominant over its allele. Its allele, on the other hand, is said to be recessive. In the case of heterozygous genes for eye color, the brown eye gene is dominant over the (recessive) blue eye gene and the offspring, therefore, will have brown eyes. Much less common is the occurrence of gene pairs in which neither gene is completely dominant over the other. This is known as INCOMPLETE or PARTIAL DOMINANCE, and results in a blending of the opposing influences. In cattle, if a homozygous (pure) red bull is mated with a homozygous (pure) white cow, the calf will be roan, a blending or mixing of red and white hairs in its coat, rather than either all red or all white.

During meiosis or division of the reproductive (sperm and egg) cells, each pair of chromosomes splits, and one-half of each pair goes into one of the two new cells. Thus, in the case of eye color genes, one new reproductive cell will get the chromosome carrying the blue eye gene, while the other new reproductive cell will get the chromosome carrying the brown eye gene, and so on for each pair of chromosomes. If an organism has only two pairs of chromosomes—called pair A made up of chromosomes A_1 and A_2, and pair B made up of chromosomes B_1 and B_2—each new reproductive cell will get one chromosome from each pair and thus four different combinations are possible: A_1 and B_1, A_1 and B_2, A_2 and B_1, or A_2 and B_2. If the blue eye gene is on A_1, the brown eye gene on A_2, and the gene for curly hair on B_1 and the gene for straight hair on B_2, each of the aforementioned combinations will exert a different genetic effect on the offspring. This different grouping of chromosomes in the new reproductive cells as a result of meiotic cell division is known as INDEPENDENT ASSORTMENT and is one reason why variation occurs in the offspring. In the dog, with thirty-nine pairs of chromosomes, the possibilities of variation through independent assortment are tremendous.

But variation does not end here. If, for example, the brown eye color gene occurred on the same chromosome as the gene for curly hair, all brown-eyed people would have curly hair. Yet in instances where such joined or LINKED genes do occur, the two characteristics do not always appear together in the same offspring. This is due to a process known as CROSSING-OVER or RECOMBINATION. Recombination is the mutual exchange of corresponding blocks of genes between the two chromosomes in a pair. That is, during cell division, the two chromosomes may exchange their tip sections or other corresponding segments. If the segments exchanged contain the eye color genes, the brown eye gene will be transferred from the chromosome carrying the curly hair gene to the chromosome carrying the straight hair gene, and then brown eyes will occur with straight hair.

Another important source of variation is MUTATION. In mutation, a gene becomes altered, such as by exposure to irradiation, and exerts a different effect than it did before. Most mutations are harmful to the organism, and some may result in death. Offspring carrying mutated genes and showing the effects of these mutations are known as MUTANTS or SPORTS. Mutation also means that instead of only two alleles for eye color, such as brown and blue, there may now be three or more (gray, black, etc.) creating a much larger source for possible variation in the offspring.

Further complications in the transmission and appearance of

genetic traits are the phenomena known as EPISTASIS and PLEIOTROPY. Epistasis refers to a gene exerting influence on genes other than its own alleles. In all-white, red-eyed (albino) guinea pigs, for example, the gene controlling intensity of color is epistatic to any other color gene and prevents that gene from producing its effect. Thus, even if a gene for red spots were present in the cells of the guinea pig, the color intensity gene would prevent the red spots from appearing in the guinea pig's white coat. Pleiotropy refers to the fact that a single gene may control a number of characteristics. In the fruit fly, for example, the gene that controls eye color may also affect the structure of certain body parts and even the lifespan of the insect.

One special pair of chromosomes is known as the sex chromosomes. In man, the dog, and other mammals, these chromosomes are of two types, designated as X and Y. Under normal conditions, a mammal carrying two X-type sex chromosomes is a female, whereas a mammal carrying one X-type and one Y-type is a male. Females, therefore, having only X chromosomes, can only contribute X chromosomes to the offspring, but the male may contribute either an X or a Y. If the male's sperm carrying an X chromosome fertilizes the female egg cell (X), the offspring (XX) will be a female; if a sperm carrying a Y chromosome fertilizes the egg (X), the offspring (XY) will be a male. It is the male, therefore, that determines the sex of the offspring in mammals.

Traits or characteristics controlled by genes present on the sex chromosome, and which appear in only one sex, are said to be *sex-linked*. If, for example, a rare recessive gene occurs on the X chromosome, it cannot exert its effect in the female because the dominant allele on the other X chromosome will counteract it. In the male, however, there is no second X chromosome, and if the Y chromosome cannot offer any counter-effect, the recessive character will appear. There are also *sex-limited* characteristics: these appear primarily or solely in one sex, but the genes for these traits are not carried on the sex chromosomes. Sex-limited traits appear when genes on other chromosomes exert their effect in the proper hormonal (male or female) environment. This is how a trait may skip a generation, by being transmitted from grandfather to grandson through a mother in which the trait, though present, does not show.

In dealing with the simplest form of heredity—one pair of genes affecting one character—there is an expected ratio of the offspring displaying the character to those who do not display it, depending upon the genetic makeup of the parents. If a parent is homozygous for a character, such as blue eyes, it makes no difference which half of the chromosome pair enters the new reproductive cell, because each chromosome carries the gene for blue eyes. If a parent is heterozygous, however, one reproductive cell will receive the brown eye gene while the other will receive the blue eye gene. If both parents are homozygous for blue eyes, all the offspring will receive two blue eye genes, and will have blue eyes. If one parent is homozygous for blue eyes, and the other parent is homozygous for brown eyes, all the offspring will be heterozygous, receiving one brown eye gene and one blue eye gene, and because brown is dominant, all will have brown eyes. If both parents are heterozygous, both the blue eye gene and the brown eye gene from one parent have an equal likelihood of ending up with either the blue eye or the brown eye gene from the other parent. This results in a ratio of two heterozygous offspring to one homozygous for brown eyes and one homozygous for blue eyes, giving a total genetic or GENOTYPIC ratio of 2:1:1, or as it is more commonly arranged, 1:2:1. As the two heterozygous offspring as well as the homozygous brown eye offspring will have brown eyes, the ratio of brown eyes to blue eyes (or PHENOTYPIC ratio) will be 3:1.

If one parent is heterozygous and the other parent homozygous for the recessive gene (as blue eyes), half of the offspring will be homozygous for blue eyes and will have blue eyes, but the other half of the offspring will be heterozygous and have brown eyes. Here both the genotypic (gene type) and phenotypic (appearance) ratio is 1:1.

If the homozygous parent, however, has the dominant gene (brown eyes), half of the offspring will be heterozygous and half will be homozygous, as before, but all will have brown eyes.

By repeated determinations of the ratios in the offspring, geneticists are able to analyze the genetic makeup of the parents.

BREEDING TERMS

Before leaving heredity, it might be well to explain the difference between inbreeding, outcrossing, linebreeding, and similar terms. Basically, there are only inbreeding and outbreeding. Inbreeding, however, according to its intensity, is usually divided into inbreeding proper and linebreeding. Inbreeding proper is considered to be the mating of very closely related individuals, generally within the immediate family, but this is sometimes extended to include first cousins and grandparents. Linebreeding is the mating of more distantly related animals, that is, animals not immediately related to each other but having a common ancestor, such as the same grandsire or great-grandsire. Outbreeding is divided into outcrossing, which is the mating of dogs from different families within the same breed; crossbreeding, which is the mating of purebred dogs from different breeds; and backcrossing, which is the mating of a crossbred animal back to one of its purebred parents or to another animal of the same strain or breed (so as to have the same genetic composition) as the purebred parent.

From the foregoing discussion of genetics, it should be realized that the theory of telegony, which states that the sire of one litter can influence future litters sired by other studs, is simply not true. It is possible, however, if several males mate with a female that the various puppies in the litter may have different sires (but not two sires for any one puppy). It should also be realized that *blood* does not really enter into the transmission of inheritance, although people commonly speak of "bloodlines," "pure-blooded," etc.

FALSE PREGNANCY

At the end of the estrous cycle, all female dogs unless actually pregnant, enter into a period of pseudo- or false pregnancy. This condition is caused by hormone-secreting structures of the ovary, known as corpora lutea, which in most other female mammals, but not the bitch, normally degenerate when ovulation is not followed by pregnancy. As a result of the activity of these persistent corpora lutea, the pseudo-pregnant dog resembles, to varying but generally much lesser degrees, the truly pregnant female in physiology, anatomy, and behavior. Pseudo-pregnancy generally lasts about sixty days.

7. Care of the Mother

PREGNANCY

Pregnancy or gestation lasts from fifty-eight to sixty-five days, with an average of sixty-two or sixty-three days (nine weeks). During this period the bitch requires special care. She should be exercised regularly, but moderately—especially toward the end of her pregnancy. Her diet, which supplies her unborn puppies as well as herself, should be rich in proteins, fat, carbohydrates, minerals (especially calcium, phosphorus, and iron), and vitamins. Feed generously, usually as much as she will eat without getting fat; three meals a day, two of meat and one of milk—plus a vitamin and mineral supplement and egg yolk are recommended.

Preparatory procedures during the last few days of the bitch's pregnancy include cleansing her teats with soap and water, reducing her food intake, and being careful to prevent her from becoming constipated. If you wish, as will be mentioned in the discussion of distemper, you may take a blood sample from the bitch to determine the period of her puppies' immunity to this disease.

THE WHELPING BOX

A whelping box should be ready at least one week prior to the predicted whelping date. The whelping box should be roomy enough to hold the bitch and her expected puppies comfortably. As a minimum, it should be about six inches longer than the bitch. The sides should be high enough to keep the puppies in, but still allow the bitch easy entrance and exit. For the Alaskan Malamute, it is probably best to build three sides at least sixteen inches high, and the fourth or entrance side about six to eight inches high, with provisions for adding additional height when the puppies grow older and larger. Some breeders use whelping boxes with hinged tops, but these are not necessary. The box must remain open during the actual whelping to allow you unobstructed observation. It is a good idea to place a guard rail around the inside of the box to prevent the female from pressing a puppy against the wall and killing it. The guard rails, which should be placed about four inches above the floor of the box, can be made of smooth wooden slats two to three inches wide by one-half to one inch thick affixed to the sides with small angle irons, or of sturdy wooden dowel rods, three-quarter-inch in diameter, set between facing walls two to three inches out from the walls they are guarding. The bottom of the box should be covered with several layers of newspaper, rather than cloth which may fold over and suffocate a puppy. Newspaper not only facilitates keeping the box clean—even though the female usually eats the elimination of the young puppies—but it can also be torn to shreds at the bitch's discretion for amusement or for a nest. Newborn puppies should not be placed on any rough surface, such as concrete, for they will rub the umbilical cord raw and bloody. The whelping box should be placed in a quiet, rather dimly-lighted place where it will be free of drafts and dampness. Introduce the bitch to the whelping box and allow or induce her to spend some time in the box and, if possible, to sleep in it. This will greatly increase the likelihood of the female using the whelping box voluntarily when the time comes.

WHELPING

The earliest signs of approaching birth are restlessness and an attempt to build a nest; nest building is indicated by scratching and digging on the sofa or bed, or by scraping objects together into a pile on the bottom of a closet. The female will often refuse food during this time, and a thick stringy discharge from the vulva may be noted. Panting, which usually begins just prior to actual delivery, may appear as much as several days before the birth of the puppies. The female's body temperature usually drops below normal about twelve hours before whelping, but this may also occur as much as forty-eight hours prior to the actual delivery. If the bitch's temperature is normal, delivery is still some time off; if it is ninety-nine or one hundred degrees, it may drop further or it may rise again, and repeat this several times; if the temperature is ninety-eight degrees or less, whelping is imminent. If you wish the presence of a veterinarian, you should notify him at this time.

The bitch may prefer some other site to the whelping box, so it may be necessary to keep her in the whelping box as the time of parturition approaches.

LABOR

Labor may be considered as occurring in two stages. The first stage consists of mild, irregularly occurring contractions of the uterus, unnoticeable to the observer, which serve to dilate the cervix and vagina. Mucus may be secreted, and the female may exhibit a general feeling of discomfort. In the second stage, usually referred to as "the labor," the uterine contractions are quite pronounced and occur at regular intervals. The contractions can be felt by placing a hand on the female's abdomen, or they may even be seen bulging her sides.

In giving birth, the female will lie on her side, and curl and strain with each contraction.

The average "labor" (second stage) and delivery of the puppies lasts from three to five hours, but some dogs may complete delivery in less than an hour. Many labors last eight hours and others may take all day. If four hours have passed since the pronounced contractions and strainings have begun without the appearance of the first puppy, it is time to call for the aid of a veterinarian. Many breeders will call a veterinarian after two hours of such fruitless exertion. It is a good general rule to call the veterinarian immediately any time during labor or delivery if you feel all is not going well. It is possible that second stage labor will begin at night and you may not be sure how long the bitch has been in labor. In this event, after one additional hour has elapsed without results, call the veterinarian. If the bitch has been in second stage labor without delivery for four or more hours before you realize her condition, she will probably be exhausted and show little or no efforts. A veterinarian should be summoned immediately.

PARTURITION

Each puppy is contained within a fluid-filled sac or "water-bag"; a tube, known as the umbilical cord, passes from the puppy's umbilicus or navel to the side of the sac that closely adheres to the wall of the uterus. Nutrients and oxygen pass across this membrane, or placenta, of the sac into the umbilical cord, and finally into the puppy's bloodstream. The puppy's wastes pass the other way and are eliminated by the female. The fluid-filled sac usually ruptures and the fluid or "water" expelled before the birth of the puppy. This may occur normally as much as two hours before the puppy's birth.

Puppies are usually born head first, but tail-first, or breech, deliveries are very common. It is best to disturb the female as little as possible during whelping, but watch carefully for any sign of trouble. If the puppy has been partially delivered and then progress halts leaving the puppy's head exposed for a minute, you should carefully remove the membranes or any other obstacle to his breathing from his face, for the umbilical cord may be pinched or severed and the oxygen supply from the mother cut off. If the puppy remains partially delivered for several minutes and *no professional help is available,* grasp the puppy (using a towel for a better grip) around the head near the neck and hold it to prevent it from slipping back in when the female relaxes. If possible, without applying force, try to hold the puppy in line with the female's hind legs to reduce the angle and resistance. *Do not pull* the puppy: the wrong angle or too great a pull may injure or kill the puppy.

In the normal events of birth, the female will nip and lick off the fetal membranes clinging to the puppy, bite or sever the umbilical cord, and eat the placenta (also called the "afterbirth"). This process may seem disgusting, but it is a normal occurrence in mammals, and there is no harm in allowing the female to follow her instincts. You should, however, make a written note, not a mental one, for each placenta expelled: one for each puppy. If even one is left inside the female, internal inflammation and infection will result, leading to her death. If a placenta remains within the female after the puppy is born, and you wish to help, grasp the umbilical cord and exert a gentle steady pull. This may be done even if the umbilical cord is still attached to the puppy. Generally, if the cord is broken, the placenta will be expelled with the next puppy.

If for some reason the female is unable to properly attend to her newborn puppies, you must lend assistance. If the puppy is still within the fluid-filled sac, quickly break it and wipe the membranes from the puppy's face with a soft cloth. If the puppy is out of the sac, which is the usual occurrence, it will just be necessary to clean its face. Some females either do a poor job of cutting the umbilical cord or do not cut it short enough. If umbilical cords are left too long in length, the bitch may constantly pull at it and seriously injure the puppy. The cord, therefore, should be cut about three-quarters of an inch from the puppy's abdomen. Any scissor may be used, but a dull scissor which crushes the cord before cutting it is believed to decrease the chance of bleeding. If more than several drops of blood do appear at the end of the cut cord, tie a piece of white cotton thread around the cord about half way down its length, and then paint the cut end of the cord with iodine or a similarly good antiseptic. The cord will drop off in two or three days.

Most puppies, if they are healthy, will squeal when they are born, but silence does not necessarily mean trouble. If a newborn puppy does not start to breathe, wrap him in a towel, hold him upside down with his head toward the ground, and shake him vigorously. At each shake, mucus will flow from his nose and mouth, and when the mucus is eliminated, the puppy will usually begin to breathe. If not, keep the puppy upside down and rub his ribs briskly. If in a short time there is still no response, adminster artificial respiration by gently compressing and releasing the sides of his ribs with both hands about twenty times a minute. Every few minutes pause in this procedure to rub the puppy's ribs briskly, and then continue the artificial respiration. Mouth-to-mouth resuscitation, using your hand as a tube to transfer air to the puppy's nostrils, making sure the same hand seals the puppy's mouth to prevent air leakage, may also be used. Blow gently until the puppy's chest rises and then quickly release—about twenty times per minute. Treatment may have to be administered for half an hour or more.

Puppies are usually born at intervals of less than one hour, but as long as the spacing is regular, there is no need for worry. Puppies are often born several close together, and then a long interval followed by the birth of several more puppies. If, following the birth of the first puppy, there seems to be an undue delay in the birth of the remaining puppies, the veterinarian can inject pitocin (oxytocin) or pituitrin, which are hormone substances that speed up delivery by stimulating contractions of the uterus. These hormones also aid in milk let-down or ejection.

After the last puppy is born, or between puppies, if the interval is long enough, the female can be taken out to relieve herself. If more puppies are to come, a short walk may even speed delivery. Warm milk may also be given to the bitch between deliveries. As each puppy is born, cleaned, and dried, it can be put to nurse on the female. You may have to place the teat into the puppy's mouth. Nursing stimulates uterine contractions and facilitates later births and expulsions of placentas.

POSTPARTUM FEEDING OF BITCH

Feed the female lightly during the first twenty-four hours after delivery: warm milk or cooked cereal are satisfactory. The female may have to be coaxed into eating. If she refuses food for thirty-six hours or longer, and her temperature is above normal, call the veterinarian; infection from a retained placenta or puppy may be present.

The nursing female will need a large intake of food containing vitamins, calcium, phosphorus, iron and other supplements. The female's supply of milk—recorded as high as a gallon a day in some 50-pound bitches—is a great drain on her body's resources. Two meat meals and one milk meal per day is a good feeding schedule. Be sure that there is always water available for drinking.

The female will probably not want to leave her puppies for the first two or three days; it may take some coaxing and coercion to get her outside for ten to fifteen minutes on each of these days.

POSTPARTUM OCCURRENCES

For a few days after whelping, especially if she has consumed the placentas, the bitch will usually have frequent, large, rather loose stools of a blackish color.

For ten to twenty-one days after whelping, the bitch will show a blackish, bloody discharge from the vulva. This is the remnant of uterine bleeding and is a normal occurrence.

It is perfectly natural for the bitch to clean up the puppies' eliminations for the first two or three weeks. After this period, or if the bitch does not take on this task, more attention must be paid to sanitation and cleanliness.

ECLAMPSIA

From the time of whelping to five or six weeks after, nursing females may suddenly display a disease known as "nursing fits" or eclampsia. This is due to a shortage of calcium in the bloodstream, which affects the parathyroid glands. Symptoms are stretching and stiffening of the muscles, muscle tremors, and high temperature. The condition may be fatal. Treatment is the injection of calcium gluco-

Ch. Kiana of Klondike,
owned by Mr. & Mrs.
A. J. DuBuis.

nate into one of the bitch's veins; recovery occurs in about fifteen minutes. The recuperating female should be kept warm and quiet, and not allowed to nurse for some time. A high calcium diet during pregnancy and nursing is one means of avoiding eclampsia. A high calcium diet is important, for even if eclampsia does not appear, the drain of calcium from the female's body will leave her bones weak and brittle unless her diet can make up the loss. The use of a vitamin and mineral supplement is highly recommended.

PUPPY FORMULA

If the female dies, an emergency milk formula is needed for the puppies. Dried milks made especially for puppies may be used, human infant formula is sometimes employed, or formulas may be made at home. One such formula is twenty-two ounces of evaporated milk, eleven ounces of water, and a tablespoon of corn (Karo) syrup; another is simply to add four egg yolks and a tablespoon of corn (Karo) syrup to a quart of whole cow's milk. The formulas should be heated and fed at one hundred degrees Fahrenheit. It will probably be necessary to stroke each puppy's belly and genitals with a piece of absorbent cotton (preferably slightly moistened with warm water) to stimulate elimination, as the mother would have done with her tongue. Orphan puppies should be fed five or six times a day.

PUPPY FEEDING AND WEANING

The puppies' eyes will open about the tenth day. If their sharp claws are scratching the bitch's breasts, it would be best to clip the claws when the puppies are about ten days old. At three weeks of age, the puppies may be given a drop or two of vitamin supplement oil or cod-liver oil. Do not force the liquid into their throats, for if any should enter their lungs, pneumonia may result. The puppies should be checked for worms at about three and one-half weeks of age, and, if even one puppy is found infested, all should be wormed.

The bitch usually begins weaning the puppies when they are about three or four weeks of age by regurgitating food for them to eat. This is a good indication that it is time to start supplementary feedings for the puppies. As most breeders begin supplementary feedings (weaning) in the fourth week, anyway, the bitch may never begin the regurgitive feeding. First foods are the same formulas as orphan puppies receive, but now only a few laps a day are necessary. The puppies may have to have their lips and chins gently but repeatedly dipped into the formula before they will start to lap. Do not push the entire face into the formula or you may clog the puppy's nose. Once puppies do lap without coaxing, it may be wise to hold the saucer at chin level to prevent the puppies from walking into the saucer. By five weeks of age, the formula should supplant from one to three regular breast feedings. If formula is fed more than once a day, the morning feeding should contain puppy meal or baby cereal; the afternoon meal, crumpled bits of toast; and the evening feeding, a repeat of the morning meal. At six weeks, scraped lean beef can be added to the diet, and the puppies separated from the mother to be returned only for short nursing periods and during the night. The amount of milk, meat, and other items fed should be increased with the puppies' growth. At eight weeks, the puppies should receive four meals a day and be completely weaned from the female.

PUPPY SLEEP

Twitching and jerking while asleep are perfectly normal occurrences in puppies and no cause for alarm.

8. Health

DISTEMPER

In the past, almost any dog ailment was called "*distemper*," just as in the 18th and 19th centuries, many human diseases in certain parts of the world were labeled "*malaria*." These ailments have subsequently been more accurately diagnosed. In the case of the dog ailments, a virus was identified, by the French scientist H. Carre, in 1905, as the cause of one form of "distemper"; this form then became known as "Carre's Disease." Later other forms of distemper were more properly diagnosed as pneumonia, coccidiosis, leptospirosis, and other diseases. Modern distemper, therefore, *is* Carre's disease.

Distemper can affect various mammals including dogs, weasels, and raccoons, but the house cat and man are immune (a disease known as feline distemper is caused by another virus; there are reports, also, that humans may pick up very mild and virtually unnoticeable cases of canine distemper).

Distemper occurs throughout the world and at any time of the year, but it is more common in winter. It is most prevalent in puppies from two to twelve months of age, with seven-month-olds appearing the most susceptible.

The earliest symptoms of distemper are commonly poor appetite, listlessness, and fatigue; temperature is high, running from one hundred and three degrees to one hundred and five degrees Fahrenheit. The puppy may whine constantly; his eyes become sensitive to light and they exude a watery discharge. Crust-like accumulations may collect around the eyes. After several days, the puppy seems improved and his temperature returns to normal. This is later followed by a second rise in temperature. Thick discharge then appears at the nose and eyes; a short dry cough develops, and the dog may have muscle spasms or shiver repeatedly. Vomiting and profuse dark-colored diarrhea also occur. The puppy displays extreme thirst.

There is little you can do once the symptoms appear. Many of the symptoms, however, are caused by bacteria rather than the distemper virus; other diseases may also follow in the wake of distemper. Veterinary help, therefore, can reduce or eliminate the bacteria and the secondary diseases and increase your dog's chances of survival. An early veterinary diagnosis may also save the lives of other dogs that have been in contact with the infected animal.

The safest course to pursue is one of prevention. There are a number of excellent distemper vaccines available. *If the mother is immune,* young puppies will receive temporary immunity while still within the mother's body and also from her colostrum or "first milk" during the first twenty-four hours of their lives. It is this temporary immunity, which may last as long as sixteen weeks, that prevents successful vaccination of young puppies. Though it is not necessary to immunize such puppies, many people like to insure immunity by having the veterinarian administer temporary "puppy shots" of homologous serum (the watery part of the blood from another dog, containing antibodies) every nine to fourteen days. Indeed, this may be the wisest course, for the puppy's immunity may not last as long as sixteen weeks. A more certain approach, however, is to take a blood sample from the bitch within a day or two of whelping. This can then be measured scientifically to ascertain how long the puppies' temporary immunity will last. When this time interval has passed, the puppies can receive their permanent vaccine.

Researchers at Cornell University, New York, report marked success with a still experimental heterotypic vaccine for puppies. Heterotypic vaccines are vaccines made from other kinds of virus than those causing the disease. In this instance, the heterotypic distemper vaccine is made from human measles virus. The advantage of the heterotypic vaccine is that, because it contains no distemper viruses, it is effective even if the puppy has colostral immunity and it protects the puppy until it is old enough to receive a permanent live virus inoculation at four months.

The puppy's temporary immunity generally wears off sometime between weaning and sixteen weeks of age; it is now susceptible to distemper but old enough to receive permanent vaccine. There are two basic kinds of permanent distemper vaccines that are commonly administered by veterinarians: the *Laidlaw-Dunkin* type and the *attenuated virus* type. The Laidlaw-Dunkin type requires three dosages or "shots" about two weeks apart. The first two "shots" are of "dead" (inactivated) viruses, while the third "shot" may be of either inactivated or live viruses. Use of inactivated virus in the third "shot" is preferred, even though it makes booster "shots" necessary. The attenuated virus vaccines are made by cultivating the distemper virus in unusual hosts, such as ferrets (as in the Green distemperoid vaccine) or chicken embryos still in the egg (as in avianized distemper vaccine). This cultivation results in harmless or attenuated viruses that are, however, still capable of stimulating immunity when injected into a dog. Attenuated vaccines require only one "shot" and no boosters.

As one-fifth of all dogs receiving *permanent* distemper inocula-

Ch. Fakir of Roy-el is owned by Walter A. and Sylvia M. Corcelius. The champion was bred by Elsie A. Truchon. Sire, Erik of Roy-el; dam, Marclar's Una. Walter A. Corcelius is shown handling the champion as judge A. E. VanCourt presents ribbon. Photo by Evelyn Shafer.

tions lose their immunity after one year, however, many veterinarians feel that *all* distemper immunizations would be more certain if booster shots are given. Live virus boosters give about twelve months' protection, inactivated virus boosters give three to five months' protection (see *dual* and *3-in-1* vaccines under "hepatitis" and "leptospirosis.").

HEPATITIS

One of the diseases formerly considered "distemper" is infectious canine hepatitis. This is a highly contagious viral disease that produces inflammation of the liver and certain other tissues within the dog's body. It occurs most commonly in dogs less than eighteen months old, but it may occur at any age. Transmission of the disease is through contact, either with an infected dog or with infected saliva or urine, but may also be carried on contaminated clothing or hands.

There are apparently several varieties or phases of canine hepatitis; this results in a rather confusing array of symptoms. An apparently healthy dog may suddenly collapse and die within twenty-four hours; other dogs may display no symptoms other than high temperature. Generally, however, the disease is characterized by its sudden beginning: temperatures of 105 degrees to 106.5 degrees Fahrenheit, which later drop to 104 to 102 degrees; listlessness; loss of appetite; watery or puslike discharge from the eyes; vomiting of a yellowish liquid; diarrhea, usually with a black tar-like stool; and labored breathing.

Hyperimmune serum (watery part of blood from an immune dog) seems to be successful in treating hepatitis. It is also used as a temporary vaccine, giving protection for two to three weeks to puppies or older dogs thought to have been in contact with the disease. Longer-lasting protection may be obtained by the use of a vaccine made from inactivated virus. There is also a dual vaccine available containing live hepatitis virus and live distemper virus, which offers what appears to be permanent protection against both diseases.

LEPTOSPIROSIS

Canine leptospirosis is a bacterial disease, damaging to the liver and kidneys, transmitted to dogs by dogs and by rodents, especially rats. Transmission occurs through contact with substances contaminated by the bacteria-laden urine of an infected animal. Canine leptospirosis occurs in two different forms, but both have many symptoms in common. Certain symptoms, however, may appear either more pronounced or solely in one of the two forms. The various symptoms of leptospirosis include listlessness, loss of weight, bloody vomit and diarrhea, stiffness in the rear legs, a dark orange or brownish urine, slime formation in the mouth and on the teeth, a yellowish (jaundice) or reddish-brown coloration of the whites of the eyes, and a yellow cast (jaundice) to the lining of the mouth.

Leptospirosis can be transmitted through abrasions of the skin or through body openings.

Treatment consists of administering antibiotics, or, if necessary, blood transfusions. Treatment in the advanced stages of the disease is not effective. Dogs die in eight to ten days. If dogs recover from the disease, permanent damage may have been done to the kidneys. Dogs may also continue to carry *Leptospira* organisms in their urine for as long as six months after recovery.

Preventative vaccines, relatively new, are now available. There is a *3-in-1* vaccine combining live avianized distemper and hepatitis viruses plus killed bacteria for leptospirosis. This is given at twelve weeks of age; yearly boosters are recommended.

TO INSURE THE HEALTH OF YOUR MALAMUTE

The dog, as man, is subjected to a wide variety of diseases. No attempt will be made to discuss all the treatments or symptoms of the various diseases. If your Malamute appears ill, a veterinarian should be consulted.

It is of utmost importance, however, to have your dog inoculated against distemper and canine hepatitis; the mortality rate of these widely prevalent diseases is extremely high in young puppies.

Your veterinarian can best determine the proper vaccination schedule for your puppy.

WORMING

Dogs are subjected to a large variety of parasitic worms. As these organisms can severely debilitate a puppy, it is wise to have your puppy examined for their presence. This is done by a veterinarian who performs a microscopic examination of the puppy's stool. If the presence of worms is indicated, the veterinarian will prescribe the proper treatment.

9. Showing

ENTERING A SHOW

To enter your Alaskan Malamute or another breed of dog in an A. K. C. approved show, your dog must be registered or eligible for registration by that organization (write to the A. K. C. for exceptions to this rule), and be at least six months old. An entry blank must be completed—giving information as to breed and sex of dog, the show class or classes in which he is to be entered, the dog's sire and dam, etc.—and then submitted with an entry fee.

The five regular classes are: *puppy class,* for American-or-Canadian-born dogs between six and twelve months of age; *novice class,* for dogs six months and older, which have never won first prize in any class other than the puppy class and which have won less than three times in the novice class itself; *bred-by-exhibitors class,* for dogs, other than champions, six months and older owned by the person who owned or leased the dog's mother at the time of her mating; *American-bred class,* for dogs, other than champions, six months and older, who were conceived and born in the United States; and the *open class,* for all dogs six months and older, including champions, but champions are rarely entered in this class today.

No more than five points may be earned in any one show. A total of fifteen points, won under at least three different judges, is required to make a dog a champion. Part of this total must consist of at least two "majors," (three or more points at a single show) awarded by two different judges.

OFFICIAL ALASKAN MALAMUTE DESCRIPTION AND STANDARD

ORIGIN: The Alaskan Malamute is a native sled-dog of Alaska and is the oldest native dog known to that country. It was originally named "Mahlemut" after a native Innuit (Mahlemut) tribe.

GENERAL APPEARANCE AND CHARACTERISTICS: A large-size dog with a strong, compact body, not too short coupled; thick dense, coarse coat and not too long; stands well over pads and

When selecting your Alaskan Malamute inquire as to what inoculations have been given.

has appearance of much activity; broad head, ears erect and wedge shaped; muzzle not too pointed and long, but not too stubby (other extreme); deep chest, proud carriage, head erect and eyes alert. Face markings are a distinguishing feature and the eyes are well set off by these markings, which consist of either cap over head and rest of face solid color (usually grayish white) or face marked with appearance of a mask, thus setting off eyes; tail is plumed and carried over the back when not working, but not too tightly curled, more like a plume waving.

Malamutes are of various colors, but usually wolfish gray or black and white. Their feet are of the "snow shoe" type with well-cushioned pads giving firm and compact appearance; front legs straight and with big bone; hind legs well bent at stifles and without cowhocks; straight back gently sloping from shoulders to hips;

endurance and intelligence are shown in body and eyes; the eyes have a "wolf-like" appearance by position of eyes, but the expression is soft; quick in action, but no loss of energy in moving; affectionate dispositions.

HEAD: The head should indicate a high degree of intelligence—it should be in proportion to the size of the dog so as not to make the dog appear clumsy or coarse. SKULL—broad between ears, gradually narrowing to eyes; moderately rounded between ears, flattening on top as it approaches eyes, round off to cheeks, which should be moderately flat. There should be a slight furrow between the eyes; the top line of the skull and top line of the muzzle showing but little break downward from a straight line as they join.

MUZZLE: Large and bulky in proportion to size of skull—diminishing but little in width or depth from junction with skull to nose—lips close fitting—nose black—upper and lower jaws broad with large teeth—the front teeth meeting with a scissors grip, but never "overshot."

EYES: Almond shaped—dark in color—moderately large for this shape of eye—set obliquely in skull.

EARS: Medium—upper half of ear triangular in shape—slightly rounded at tips—set wide apart on outside back edges of top of skull with lower part of ear joining the skull on a line with the upper corner of eye; giving the tips of the ears the appearance, when erect, of standing off from the skull; when erect, ears are pointed slightly forward, but when at work the ears are usually folded back against the skull.

BODY: Chest should be strong and deep; body should be strong and compactly built, but not too short coupled; the back should be straight and gently sloping from shoulders to hips. Loins well muscled, but no surplus weight.

SHOULDERS, LEGS AND FEET: Shoulders moderately sloping; fore legs heavily boned and muscled—straight to pasterns, which should be short and strong and almost vertical as viewed from the side; feet large and compact, toes well arched, pads thick and tough, toe nails short and strong; protective growth of hair between toes. Hind legs must be broad and powerfully muscled through thighs; stifles moderately bent, hock joints broad and strong and moderately bent and well let down—as viewed from behind, the hind legs should not appear bowed in bone, but stand and move true and not too close or too wide. The legs of the Malamute must indicate unusual strength and powerful propelling power—any definite indication of unsoundness in legs and feet, standing or moving, constitutes practically disqualification in the show ring.

COAT: Thick, dense, coarse coat, but not long, under coat is thick, oily and woolly, while outer coat is rather coarse and stands

Alaskan Malamutes seem always to have that alert expression.

out. Thick fur around neck. (This allows for protection against weather.)

COLOR AND MARKINGS: The usual colors are wolfish gray or black and white. Markings should be either cap-like or mask-like on face. A variation of color and markings is occasionally found.

TAIL: Well furred and carried over back when not working, but not too tightly curled to rest on back, a "waving plume" appearance instead.

HEIGHT: Of male dog, averaging from twenty-two to twenty-five inches; of bitch, averaging from twenty to twenty-three inches.

WEIGHT: Of male dog, averaging from sixty-five to eighty-five pounds; of bitch, averaging from fifty to seventy pounds.

Note the proper tail carriage of this Alaskan Malamute.

SCALE OF POINTS:	POINTS
General appearance	20
Head	20
Body	20
Legs and feet	20
Coat and color	10
Tail	10
TOTAL	100

HANDLERS

Many breeders employ professional handlers to exhibit their dogs. The advantages of a professional handler are twofold: many breeders do not have the time or finances to travel from show to show to give their dogs the opportunity to earn championships or coveted awards so vital to the success of a kennel; the professional handler's experience in knowing how to show your dog to its best advantage. Handling your own dog, however, can bring added joy, interest, and excitement in owning your dog, as well as introducing you to the international community of dogdom.

Ch. Kobuk's Manassas
Mischief,   owned by
Mr. & Mrs. A. J. DuBuis.

BIBLIOGRAPHY

Breed Your Dog, Dr. Leon Whitney, 64 pp.,   Illustrated throughout
with instructive photographs in both color and black and white. Covers
aspects of breeding through puppyhood.

Dollars In Dogs, Leon F. Whitney, D.V.M., 255 pp.,   Twenty-six
chapters on different vocations in the vast field of dog business. An excellent book for your library.

First Aid For Your Dog, Dr. Herbert Richards, 64 pp.,   Illustrated
throughout in both color and black and white.

Groom Your Dog, Leon F. Whitney, D.V.M., 64 pp.,   Illustrated
throughout with both color and black and white photographs showing
various grooming techniques.

How To Feed Your Dog, Dr. Leon F. Whitney, 64 pp.,   Best diets and feeding routines for puppies and adult canines. Profusely illustrated in color and black and white.

How To Housebreak And Train Your Dog, Arthur Liebers, 80 pp., Six educational chapters on training your dog. Illustrated in color and black and white photographs.

How To Raise And Train A Pedigreed Or Mixed Breed Puppy, Arthur Liebers, 64 pp.,   Nine chapters covering such canine questions as choosing your puppy through breeding the adult. Illustrated in both color and black and white photographs.

How To Show Your Dog, Virginia Tuck Nichols, 252 pp.,   This book is written for the novice who plans to show his dog. An excellent text to make your dog library complete.

The Distemper Complex, Leon F. Whitney, D.V.M., and George D. Whitney, D.V.M., 219 pp.,   A comprehensive canine health book. Nineteen revealing chapters. A thirty-nine-page bibliography. Completely indexed.

This Is The Puppy, Ernest Hart, 190 pp.,   Eleven profusely-illustrated chapters to guide the reader in the care and selection of a puppy. Full-color photographs. Also black and white candids. Indexed.

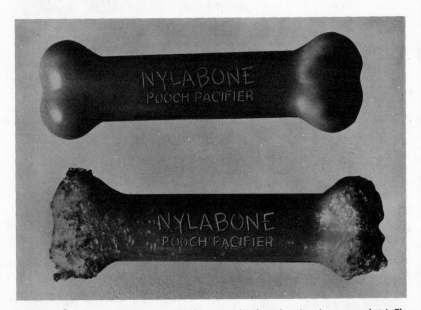

NYLABONE® is a necessity that is available at your local petshop (not in supermarkets). The puppy or grown dog chews the hambone flavored nylon into a frilly dog toothbrush, massaging his gums and cleaning his teeth as he plays. Veterinarians highly recommend this product . . . but beware of cheap imitations which might splinter or break.